Exceptional
African Americans

PHILLIS WHEATLEY

*Colonial
African-American
Poet*

Charlotte Taylor

Enslow Publishing
101 W. 23rd Street
Suite 240
New York, NY 10011
USA

enslow.com

Words to Know

abandon—To leave without planning to come back.

asthma—A condition that affects the lungs and can make it difficult for someone to breathe.

colony—An area that is ruled by another country.

culture—The beliefs, practices, art, and faiths of a group of people.

debtor—A person who owes someone money.

historian—A person who studies the past.

kidnapped—Having been carried off by force.

publish—To produce a book or magazine so people can read it.

Contents

PHILLIS WHEATLEY, NEGRO SERVANT to Mr. JOHN WHEATLEY, of BOSTON.

Phillis Wheatley

CHAPTER 1

Kidnapped

In 1761 a seven-year-old girl was taken from her home in Africa. Many other African people were **kidnapped** as well. The little girl and the others were taken by white men who would sell them as slaves in the American **colonies**. The men put the Africans on large ships. The ships were crowded with men and women, boys and girls.

The boat sailed across the Middle Passage. This was a route used by slave ships to travel from Africa to the Americas. The conditions on the ships were terrible. The Africans were tightly packed together.

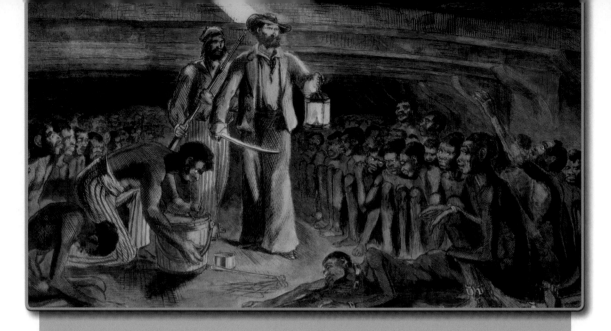

As a young girl, Phillis traveled on a slave ship from Africa to America. It was a long voyage and the people were packed tightly together. Many got sick and died.

It was dark and hot. The African people wore heavy chains. They could not move very much. They had very little to eat or drink.

A New Life

The ship finally reached Boston. The young girl was sold at a slave auction. She was very weak. All she wore was a piece of dirty carpet. She was missing two front teeth.

She was bought by John and Susannah Wheatley. The Wheatleys had a son and a daughter named Nathaniel and Mary. The Wheatleys did not know the little girl's name. She could not tell them because she did not speak English. They named her Phillis. It was the name of the slave ship.

Phillis was too sick to work hard in the house. But she was very smart. The Wheatleys' daughter, Mary, taught Phillis to speak English. She taught Phillis to read and write English, too. She also taught her to read Latin. Phillis worked very hard at her lessons. Soon she could read the Bible. Mrs. Wheatley was very happy to see Phillis learn so quickly.

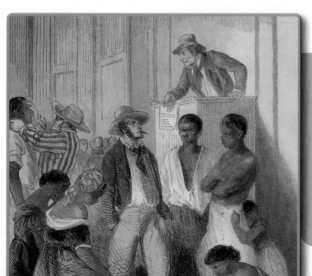

Once slaves arrived in America, they were sold at auctions like this one. Families were often separated and sold to different owners.

Phillis Says:

"I, young in life, by seeming cruel fate Was snatch'd from Afric's fancy'd happy seat."

The Wheatley family lived in Boston, Massachusetts. Many ships carrying captured Africans sailed into Boston Harbor, where they were sold as slaves.

CHAPTER 2

Phillis the Poet

Life was very difficult for most slaves. Most white people thought that Africans were not as good as them. They did not understand that Africans had a different **culture** from Americans. Many slaves were treated like animals. White Americans were impressed by Phillis. Because she could read and write, she was treated better than most slaves.

Phillis soon began to write poetry. She wrote about religion. She wrote about people she met and things she saw. She wrote about famous people, like King George of England. Mrs. Wheatley liked

Many slaves worked hard from morning until night and were often whipped if they disobeyed their master.

her poetry. She encouraged Phillis to keep writing. In some ways, the Wheatleys treated her like a member of the family. They were very proud of her. But she was still a slave.

Phillis Proves Herself

Many white people didn't believe Phillis could write poems. They thought people with dark skin were not smart. Famous white people had written articles about black people. They said people with dark skin were a different species from white people.

Mr. Wheatley wanted to prove that Phillis was very smart. He wanted to show the world that she had written her own poems. He arranged for a group of men in Boston to question Phillis. They

Phillis wrote poetry about people she admired, like Reverend George Whitefield, seen here. Her poem about him, written after his death, was published in many newspapers.

included the governor of Massachusetts, John Hancock, and church leaders. They decided that her intelligence was real.

Phillis Says:

"Some view our sable race with scornful eye, 'Their colour is a diabolic die.' Remember, Christians, Negro's, black as Cain, May be refin'd, and join th' angelic train."

Many white people thought that Africans were not as smart as they were. They thought that it was acceptable to treat black people as if they did not have the same feelings and thoughts.

CHAPTER 3
Success for Phillis

In the 1770s Massachusetts was a British colony. American colonists had to pay taxes to England for many goods. They were unhappy with the British rules. The colonists were ready to fight for freedom from Britain. The American Revolution was coming. Phillis wrote about the ideas of the Revolution in her poetry.

Phillis wrote many poems. Mrs. Wheatley had arranged for them to be **published**. Then Phillis wrote a book of poetry. No one in Boston would publish it because it was written by a slave. The Wheatleys sent a copy of Phillis's book to London. Archibald Bell agreed to publish it there. It would have a picture of Phillis on the front. People would know she was black.

American colonists were becoming very unhappy with British rule. On March 5, 1770, British soldiers fired into a crowd of colonists, killing five people. The Boston Massacre brought America a step closer to war with England.

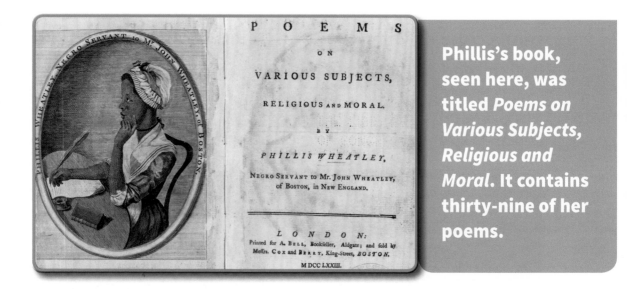

Phillis's book, seen here, was titled *Poems on Various Subjects, Religious and Moral.* It contains thirty-nine of her poems.

Free at Last

Phillis's book was being published in London. She and Nathaniel Wheatley sailed there. The sea air was good for her **asthma**, which sometimes made it hard for her to breathe. Phillis met many celebrities in London. Even King George wanted to meet her. When Phillis returned to Boston, the Wheatleys freed her. She was no longer a slave!

Nathaniel Wheatley went with Phillis on her trip to London in 1773. The British people were more willing to accept a black poet than those back home in America.

Phillis Says:

"Imagination! Who can sing thy force? Or who describe the swiftness of thy course?"

CHAPTER 4
Final Years

The years that followed were not easy ones. Over the next ten years, all of the Wheatleys died. The family had helped Phillis a great deal. She was very sad. But she also had happier times. She sent George Washington a poem she had written about him. He was impressed and invited her to visit him.

Phillis met John Peters, another freed slave. They were married in 1778. John struggled to make ends meet. They sank into terrible poverty. Two of Phillis's three children died. John **abandoned** her. Some **historians** think he went to **debtor's** prison.

After George Washington read Phillis's poem about him, he invited her to visit him at his home. She accepted his invitation and met with him in 1776.

Phillis became very poor. She could not sell another book. She died in 1784, at the age of thirty-one. Her third child died the same day. Nobody knows for sure where Phillis is buried. Being black in a white world took its toll, but Phillis was brave. She lives on today through her poetry.

Phillis Says:

"Restrain the sorrow streaming from thine eye, Be all thy future moments crown'd with joy!"

Today this monument to Phillis Wheatley stands in Boston. It reminds people of the young woman who found success even when most people thought it was impossible.

Timeline

1761—Phillis Wheatley arrives in Boston from West Africa. She is sold as a slave to the Wheatley family.

1767—Phillis's first poem is published.

1771—Phillis joins Boston's Old South Church.

1773—Phillis is freed by the Wheatleys.
Phillis travels to England.
Phillis's book of poetry is published. It is the first book of poetry written by an African American.

1774—Mrs. Wheatley dies.

1778—Mr. Wheatley and Mary Wheatley die.

Phillis marries John Peters.

1784—Phillis Wheatley dies.

1786—Phillis's book is first printed in America.

Learn More

Books

Aloian, Molly. *Phillis Wheatley: Poet of the Revolutionary Era*. New York: Crabtree, 2013.

Malaspina, Ann. *Phillis Sings Out Freedom: The Story of George Washington and Phillis Wheatley*. Park Ridge, IL: Albert Whitman, 2010.

Rojczak, Kristen. *Life During the American Revolution*. New York: Gareth Stevens, 2013.

Websites

www.earlyamerica.com/notable-women/phillis-wheatley/
Learn more about the life and works of Phillis Wheatley.

www.poemhunter.com/phillis-wheatley/
Read a selection of poems by Phillis Wheatley.

Index

Published in 2016 by Enslow Publishing, LLC.
101 W. 23rd Street, Suite 240, New York, NY 10011

Library of Congress Cataloging-in-Publication Data
Taylor, Charlotte, 1978-
  Phillis Wheatley : colonial African-American poet / Charlotte Taylor.
    pages cm. — (Exceptional African Americans)
 Summary: "Describes the life and work of colonial poet Phillis Wheatley"— Provided by publisher.
 Includes bibliographical references and index.
 ISBN 978-0-7660-7326-5 (library binding)
 ISBN 978-0-7660-7324-1 (pbk.)
 ISBN 978-0-7660-7325-8 (6-pack)
1. Wheatley, Phillis, 1753-1784—Juvenile literature. 2. Poets, American—Colonial period, ca. 1600-1775—Biography—Juvenile literature. 3. African American women poets—Biography—Juvenile literature. 4. Slaves—United States—Biography—Juvenile literature. I. Title.
 PS866.W5Z698 2016
 811'.1—dc23
 [B]
                  2015026935

Printed in the United States of America

To Our Readers: We have done our best to make sure all website addresses in this book were active and appropriate when we went to press. However, the author and the publisher have no control over and assume no liability for the material available on those websites or on any websites they may link to. Any comments or suggestions can be sent by e-mail to customerservice@enslow.com.

Photo Credits: Throughout book, © Toria/Shutterstock.com (blue background); cover, pp. 1, 4 Culture Club/Hulton Archive/Getty Images; pp. 6, 7, 19 Everett Historical/Shutterstock.com; p. 8 J. Carwitham/Yale Center for British Art/Wikimedia Commons/East View of the City of Boston in North America/public domain; p. 10 Library of Congress Prints and Photographs Division; p. 11 Hulton Archive/Getty Images; p. 13 Universal History Archive/UIG/Getty Images; p. 15 Stock Montage/Archive Photos/Getty Images; p. 16 MPI/Archive Photos/Getty Images; p. 17 DEA/G.Nimatallah/De Agostini/Getty Images; p. 21 Education Images/UIG via Getty Images.